ONE

Hi! My name's **Nelson Kane** . . .
also known as **NINJA KID!**

I got my **ninja powers** from my dad, who went missing when I was just a baby. For years, my father's disappearance was a mystery. But I think I've finally worked it out.

Dr Kane, my dad's evil twin brother, put a microchip in Dad's neck and transformed him into the **ULTIMATE NINJA**.

NINJA KID 8

NINJA DOGS!

Scholastic Press
An imprint of Scholastic Australia Pty Limited (ABN 11 000 614 577)
PO Box 579 Gosford NSW 2250
www.scholastic.com.au

Part of the Scholastic Group
Sydney • Auckland • New York • Toronto • London • Mexico City
• New Delhi • Hong Kong • Buenos Aires • Puerto Rico

First published by Scholastic Australia in 2021.
Text copyright © Anh Do, 2021.
Illustrations by Anton Emdin and Jeremy Ley, 2021.
Anh Do asserts his moral rights as the author of this work.
Anton Emdin and Jeremy Ley assert their moral rights as the illustrators of this work.

All rights reserved. No part of this publication may be reproduced in whole or in part or transmitted in any form or by any means, electronic or mechanical, including photocopying, recording, storage in an information retrieval system, or used to train any artificial intelligence technologies, or otherwise without the prior written permission of the publisher, unless specifically permitted under the Australian Copyright Act 1968 as amended.

ISBN 978-93-5471-933-2

A catalogue record for this book is available from the National Library of Australia

Typeset in Bizzle-Chizzle, featuring Hola Bisou and Handblock.

This reprint edition: November 2025

Printed in India at MicroPrints India, New Delhi

ANH DO

illustrated by Anton Emdin

NINJA KID 8

NINJA DOGS!

A Scholastic Press book
from Scholastic Australia

One day, I'm going to remove that microchip and bring my dad home.

Home is a junkyard in Duck Creek where I live with my mum, Grandma and my cousin Kenny, who is always **hungrier than a hippo!**

Duck Creek used to be the **quietest** town ever. But lately, it's been constantly under attack from Dr Kane.

When Dr Kane wages war on Duck Creek, I turn into **NiNJA KiD** and Kenny turns into my super **sidekick**, **H-DUDE**.

So far, we've managed to **fend off** every one of Dr Kane's attacks. But H-Dude and I couldn't save Duck Creek on our own. We get plenty of help from our friends, Sarah and Tiffany, who don't need superhero costumes to do **heroic** things.

And we'd be useless without Grandma's `incredible inventions`. Grandma is so ahead of her time, she creates things people don't even know they need yet!

OK, sometimes Grandma's inventions go a little off the rails.

Like the robotic paintbrush, which can paint a whole house in under an hour . . .

. . . if you can get it to stop chasing you!

Or the clever underpants, which know the answer to any question. Trouble is, they sometimes yell out **random facts** at the wrong time!

Grandma has invented some remarkable things, but her latest invention might just be her **greatest ever . . .**

TWO

'Cool bracelet, Grandma,' I said.

'When did you move into fashion?' Kenny asked.

'It's got nothing to do with fashion,' Grandma replied. 'It's a dog transformation bracelet.'

'To put it simply,' Grandma said, 'this bracelet can turn you into a dog.'

'What?!' I exclaimed.

'No way!' Kenny added.

'What sort of dog?' I asked.

'Whichever breed you're thinking about when the bracelet **ZAPS** you,' Grandma replied.

Kenny and I stared at Grandma in shock!

'You're an incredible inventor, Grandma,' I said. 'But turning a human into a dog is **impossible**.'

'Nothing's impossible,' Grandma said. 'Now, which one of you brave young men will be my guinea pig?'

Kenny grabbed my hand and thrust it into the air.

'Thank you, Nelson,' Grandma said.

'**Hey!**' I replied.

But it was too late, Grandma was leading me outside.

'Right,' Grandma said. 'Nelson, I need you to **focus** on the dog breed you want to become.'

'Forever?!' I asked.

'Of course not,' Grandma said. 'I can turn you back into a human whenever you like.'

'Okaaay . . .' I replied nervously.

Grandma's index finger hovered over a shiny silver button in the middle of the bracelet. 'Are you thinking about a dog breed, Nelson?' she asked.

'Yep!' I replied, in a high-pitched voice.

'Which breed?' Kenny asked.

'Let's keep it a surprise,' Grandma said. 'Ready, Nelson?'

'I . . . guess.'

'Excellent!' Grandma said.

ZAP!

I felt strange. **Really** strange. It didn't help that Kenny was rolling around on the grass, laughing.

Grandma wasn't laughing. She was studying me curiously.

I looked down. I now had Scottish terrier paws and a Scottish terrier tummy, just like I'd imagined.

Wow, the transformation has been a huge success, I thought . . .

Until Grandma held up a mirror!

'You're half terrier, half bulldog,' said Kenny. **'You're Terribull!'**

'What went wrong?' I asked Grandma. I was relieved that I could still talk!

'I just need to make a few tiny tweaks,' Grandma replied.

As she fiddled with the bracelet, Kenny held up a big stick. **'Fetch, Nelson!'** he called and threw the stick into the grass.

'I am definitely **not** chasing that,' I said. But before I knew it, I'd grabbed the stick in my mouth!

'Let's try again, Nelson,' Grandma said. 'Think of a **different dog breed** this time.'

'Wouldn't it be safer to just turn me back into a human?' I asked.

'Not yet,' Grandma said. 'We're on the verge of greatness. Three, two, one . . .'

I felt even stranger this time. And Kenny was **laughing** even harder.

I stared down at myself . . .

I had a **boxer** body and paws, just like I'd imagined.

Grandma studied me curiously then held the mirror up again.

'Unbelievable!' laughed Kenny. 'This time you're a cross between a **poodle** and a **boxer**.'

Grandma kept TWEAKING and **ZAPPING** but things weren't improving.

Finally, Grandma got the bracelet to work perfectly.

'I knew we'd get there in the end,' Grandma said.

'You look very handsome as a **collie!**' Kenny joked.

'Thanks,' I said. 'Grandma, can I go back to being regular old Nelson now?'

'I hope so,' Grandma said, tinkering with the bracelet again.

She wasn't exactly filling me with confidence!

'Stand still, Nelson.

I looked down . . .

I had human hands. Human legs. And everything else was human.

I was Nelson Kane again!

'That was super impressive, Grandma!' Kenny exclaimed.

'Thanks for volunteering, Nelson,' Grandma said. 'Kenny, you can be the guinea pig for my **dinosaur bracelet**.'

Kenny's eyes almost popped out of his head. 'Have you **really** invented a dinosaur bracelet?!'

'Well, it's on my "To-Do" list,' Grandma said.

Kenny and I couldn't help imagining what we'd look like as **dinosaurs**.

'I have to go to the hardware store,' Grandma said. 'Promise me you two **won't** touch the bracelet unless it's an absolute **emergency.**'

'We promise,' I said.

'Emergency use only,' Kenny said.

But when Grandma put the bracelet back in the workshop, Kenny winked at me!

THREE

Grandma had only just driven out of the junkyard when Kenny rushed into her workshop and retrieved the dog bracelet.

'Did you hear a word of what Grandma just said?!' I asked.

'Yeah, I heard **all the words,**' Kenny replied.

'So you know the bracelet is **only** for emergencies.'

'But you saw how unpredictable this bracelet is,' Kenny said. 'We need to **practise** so when an emergency comes, we're ready.'

Kenny was awesome at making **bad ideas** seem like **good** ones!

'I don't know . . .' I said nervously.

'Grandma's always telling us how important **preparation** is,' Kenny replied. 'Let's just do a quick test run!'

'Super quick!' I said. 'And I get to wear the bracelet first!'

'Dealio!' Kenny replied, handing over the bracelet.

'OK, think of a dog breed,' I said.

'One step ahead of you!' Kenny replied.

'Excellent. Three, two, one . . .'

Kenny had transformed into a **Great Dane!**

'How do you feel?' I asked.

'GREAT!' Kenny replied. 'Except now I'm even hungrier than I was before. Hey, is that a bone?'

Kenny ***pounced*** on the bone and chewed it like he'd been a dog forever!

'Alright, Kenny,' I said. 'Time to **ZAP** you back.'

'**Wait!** Let's both be dogs for a little while. Put the bracelet on my paw!'

'What happened to this being a super-quick practice session?' I asked.

'I haven't had a go with the bracelet yet,' Kenny said. '**I'm** not prepared for an emergency.'

'Alright,' I said. 'Here . . .'

I put the bracelet on Kenny's paw and he aimed it at me.

'Are you thinking about a dog breed?' he asked.

'Sure am!'

'Alrighty. Three, two, one . . .'

I became a **corgi!**

I'd heard the *Queen of England* had corgis, and I liked the idea of being dog royalty!

'Nice choice!' Kenny said. 'Let's go for a dog walk, **your majesty!**'

This time, Kenny didn't even wait for me to respond before he dashed out of the junkyard gates.

I sighed, then followed after him on my tiny little legs!

As we ran down the street, everything had a stronger smell – the air, the grass, the flowers. Then there was a new odour. This one **wasn't** pleasant at all . . .

Kenny was weeing on a fire hydrant!

'That's gross, Kenny!' I exclaimed.

'A dog's gotta do what a dog's gotta do!' he replied.

We did a little more walking and sniffing until we ran into a little dog. It looked like a super-cute mixed poodle . . . **a Moodle!**

'Hello, fellow dog!' Kenny said.

The Moodle barked. And Kenny and I understood what she was saying!

'Hello,' the Moodle said in a soft voice. 'Can you help me? My owners have moved away, and I've been left all alone. I'm scared and **Soooo** hungry!'

'Why don't you come back to our place?' I said. 'You can stay with us and have something to eat until you find a new owner.'

'Really?' the Moodle said. 'That would be amazing.'

'Least we can do!' Kenny said. 'I'm Kenny, by the way. And this is Nelson.'

'I'm Noodles,' said the Moodle.

The three of us shook paws!

As we scampered back to the junkyard, Kenny whispered, 'Should we tell Noodles we're not actually dogs?'

'That might **freak her out**,' I said. 'Let's wait until she gets to know us better first.'

'I like the way you think, young corgi,' Kenny said.

We bounded into the junkyard.

'Wait here, Noodles,' I said. 'We'll get our owners to bring you some food and water.'

'And a couple of toys,' Kenny added.

'You are incredibly kind,' Noodles replied.

'We try to be **good** canine citizens!' Kenny said, and we hurried inside.

Before Mum could see us, we used the bracelet to turn ourselves back into humans!

Kenny and I made Noodles a feast fit for a king! We also poured her a big bowl of fresh water and scrounged together a basket full of dog toys.

We carried them all out to Noodles, but now we were **humans,** she didn't recognise us at all.

'You must be Noodles,' I said.

'We heard you might be a little hungry,' Kenny said.

Noodles **barked** and **wagged** her tail.

Mum spotted Noodles and hurried over to us. 'Who's this **cutey?**' she asked.

'This is Noodles,' Kenny said. 'She was lost and hungry so we brought her back to the junkyard.'

'How did you know she was lost and hungry?' Mum asked.

Kenny and I shared a **worried** look.

'Ahhhh . . . the way she was barking,' Kenny said.

'Right,' Mum said, bemused. 'And how do you know her name is Noodles? She doesn't have a name tag.'

'Um . . .' I spluttered. 'She just looks like a Noodles. Don't you think?'

'I guess,' Mum replied.

'Can we look after her until she finds a new owner?' Kenny asked.

'Please!' I added.

'Of course,' Mum said. 'There's an old kennel in the junkyard. Maybe you two can spruce it up.'

'Love to!' Kenny said.

Noodles wagged her tail excitedly again.

It was almost dark by the time Kenny and I finished fixing up the old kennel. It took a heap of work, but we were super proud of our renovation skills.

It looked like a **fancy dog hotel!** We had even made a little sign and called it *Barkingham Palace.*

Noodles loved it! She wagged her tail, curled up inside the kennel and fell fast asleep.

FOUR

As soon as Kenny and I woke up the next morning, we ran outside to see Noodles. But her kennel was **empty!**

We searched the entire junkyard. There was no sign of her **anywhere.**

Kenny and I wanted to keep searching but we were running late for school.

'I'm sure she'll **turn up** before you get home,' Mum said.

I wanted to believe Mum, but I had a **bad feeling** about it.

My bad feeling turned into a **very bad feeling** when we arrived at school and discovered everyone else's pets had gone missing, too!

'My dog, Puggy, has disappeared,' Sarah said. 'There's **no way** he could have escaped on his own. We made the backyard a fortress because Puggy's an **ESCAPE MASTER!'**

Tiffany's cat, Furball, had also **vanished** without a trace.

So had Charles' prized pony, **Fancypants.**

And Billy Bob's llama, **Wally,** was also missing.

Everyone was so worried about their pets that Mr Fletcher couldn't get us to concentrate on our schoolwork.

Finally, the home-time bell rang and it was time for the weekend. We gathered in the playground to come up with a plan to find our pets.

'Let's meet up tomorrow morning,' Tiffany said, 'and conduct a massive **group search** of Duck Creek.'

'Awesome idea,' Kenny said.

'It was actually **my** idea,' Charles said. 'Tiffany just said it before I could.'

'It doesn't matter whose idea it was,' Sarah said. 'We need to **find our pets**.'

'Should we meet outside the junkyard at nine in the morning?' I asked.

'The junkyard?' Charles said. 'Who wants to meet outside **a junkyard?!**'

'I do,' Sarah said.

'Me too,' Tiffany added.

'Me three,' Billy Bob said.

'Majority rules!' Kenny said.

'See you all outside the junkyard tomorrow at nine sharp,' I said.

The whole way home from school, Kenny and I looked for Noodles.

We searched for the other missing pets, too.

When we arrived home, the first thing we did was search the **whole junkyard** for Noodles. There was still no sign of her.

Kenny and I were now **seriously worried.**

There was something very strange going on – but what was it?

FiVE

Kenny and I hardly slept, we were so worried about Noodles and the other pets. In the morning, we gobbled down our banana pancakes and tried to rush out the door.

'Whoa, whoa, whoa!' Mum exclaimed. 'Where are you two rushing off to?'

'To find Noodles and the other missing pets,' I said.

'In that case,' Grandma said, 'take this.'

'I'm guessing you both know how to use it,' Grandma said. 'Considering you tried it out the other day, even though **I told you not to.**'

Grandma always caught us out when we did the wrong thing.

'We're so sorry, Grandma,' I said.

'It was my idea,' Kenny said. 'I thought it would be good to get some practice with the dog bracelet before an **emergency** happened.'

'That was a good idea,' Grandma said. 'All you had to do was **ask.**'

'If Grandma tells you not to touch something,' Mum said, 'please **listen** to her.'

'Thank you for apologising,' Grandma said. 'Now, **be careful** out there today. I've got a bad feeling about these missing pets.'

'Me too!' I said.

'Do you think **Dr Kane's** involved?' Kenny asked.

'Stealing pets certainly sounds like one of his evil ideas,' Grandma replied.

'Please look out for each other,' Mum said.

'We will,' Kenny said.

We headed out the door. But not before Kenny **stuffed one more** pancake in his mouth and two more in his pockets.

We met up with Charles, Billy Bob, Tiffany and Sarah outside the junkyard. Everyone was dressed in hiking clothes. Charles had all the latest gear – he looked like an ad for an **adventure shop!**

'Wow,' Charles said. 'This place is even more of a **dump** than I imagined.'

'I think it's cool,' Tiffany said.

'Me too,' Sarah added.

'Me three!' Billy Bob said.

'We appreciate your feedback,' Kenny replied.

'So, where should we start our search?' I asked.

'Puggy has a GPS tracker attached to his collar,' Sarah said. 'I've borrowed Mum's phone so I can connect to it.'

'Looks like Puggy is in the woods just outside of Duck Creek,' Sarah said.

'Urgh,' Kenny replied. 'Those woods give me the **creeps.**'

'I've heard they're haunted,' Billy Bob added.

'They're not **haunted!**' Sarah said. 'I go for walks there all the time with my mum.'

'You two better put your big-boy pants on,' Tiffany said. 'Because we're heading into the woods.'

The six of us walked quickly towards the edge of town. We were so desperate to find our animals, we hardly said a word.

As we moved into the woods, the trees grew increasingly tall. Soon, they were so **big** they were blocking the sun.

Everyone was starting to feel a little **EDGY**, even Tiffany.

'I don't know why you're all so nervous,' Charles said. 'These woods aren't scary at – **ARRGGHHH!**'

A bat flew overhead and Charles **dived** to the ground, *squealing*.

'Slick moves there, Charles,' said Kenny. 'You should be an **acro-bat!'**

'I wasn't scared,' Charles said. 'I tripped.'

As I helped Charles up, I noticed something amongst the leaves . . . a bright pink headband.

'Does anyone recognise this?' I asked.

'That's Furball's headband!' Tiffany said.

'That means we're on the right path,' I said. 'What's the tracking app saying, Sarah?'

'We're close,' Sarah said. 'Puggy seems to be on the other side of these woods.'

'Let's pick up the pace,' Tiffany said. 'Furball needs me!'

Tiffany **sprinted** through the trees.

'C'mon, everyone, **let's go!**' I said.

We all raced on ahead through the woods to keep up with Tiffany.

SiX

We kept running until we reached a dangerous-looking creek.

'This is the start of Duck Creek, where our town got its name,' I said. 'It's known for having **really dangerous** rapids.'

'The tracker shows Puggy is on the other side of the river,' Sarah said.

'Then what are we waiting for?' Tiffany asked.

She ***sprinted*** towards the creek, **soared** high above the surging waters and landed nimbly on the other side.

'That was **incredible!'** Kenny said.

'You can do it, too,' Tiffany said. 'Just make sure you get plenty of momentum.'

'I'm going to need a lot more than momentum,' Kenny said nervously.

'Coming your way!' Sarah called out to Tiffany.

Sarah started her run-up and was about to leap across the river when Charles stood in her path.

'I want to go second!' he said.

Sarah **bumped** into him and fell to the ground.

Her mum's phone **bounced** out of her hand and into the river.

'Oh no!' Tiffany exclaimed.

'Don't worry,' Sarah said. 'The phone's waterproof!'

'Not sure that's going to help much,' Kenny said.

Within seconds, the phone was sucked downstream and swept out of sight.

'Nice one, Charles!' Sarah said, upset.

'What's the **BIG deal?'** said Charles. 'Tell your mum to use a spare. My dad has ten phones.'

'That phone was the key to us **finding** our pets!' Tiffany said from the other side of the river.

'Don't blame me!' Charles said. 'Sarah was the one who dropped it.'

'We all need to be on the **same team,'** I said. 'We've found one clue that helped us know which way to go, I'm sure we'll find more.'

'And when we get home, Charles,' Kenny said, 'you need to buy Sarah's mum a new phone!'

'Whatever,' Charles grumbled.

'Right now, we need to concentrate on getting the rest of us across the river,' I said.

Sarah channelled her frustration into her jump. She leapt **high** and **long** and crossed the creek easily.

Charles and Billy Bob also made the leap with room to spare.

Kenny and I looked nervously at the moving water.

'On the count of three?' I said.

'Can we count down from four?' Kenny asked. 'I might need one more count.'

'Fine. Four, three, two, one . . .'

We soared through the air.

Our joy disappeared when we started **dropping** towards the raging rapids. We **stretched** out our legs . . . and just managed to make it to the other side.

'Nice jumping, guys!' Tiffany said.

Sarah tried to smile but I could tell she was really worried about Puggy and her mum's phone.

As we trekked through the woods, Kenny tried to **brighten the mood** with bad jokes.

'What did the tree wear to the beach?' Kenny asked.

'Swimming trunks!' Tiffany said.

'How'd you guess?' Kenny asked.

'I love tree jokes, too,' Tiffany said. 'How did the tree access the internet?'

'It logged in!' Kenny replied.

As Kenny and Tiffany swapped jokes, the rest of us kept an eye out for any more pet clues.

We trekked deeper into the woods, and it became darker and colder. We started getting a little bit scared.

'So, where are all these clues you were talking about, Nelson?' Charles sneered.

'How about **that** one?' Kenny said.

'That's Puggy's collar!' Sarah said, excitedly. She held the collar up to her cheek. 'We're going to find you super soon, little guy.'

'Whoa!' Billy Bob rushed ahead of us and picked something up. 'This is Wally's favourite top!' he said, holding up a colourful, striped jumper.

'Our pets are **leaving us clues** to help find them!' Tiffany said.

'I knew Wally was **smart,**' Billy Bob said, 'but I didn't know he was **this smart!** Wally, I'm going to bring you home, buddy!'

SEVEN

We found several more pet clues. Following them led us along the creek bank.

'Dr Kane has to be behind this,' I whispered to Kenny.

'Who else could do something so **despicable?'** Kenny replied.

'What are you two whispering about?' Charles said.

'We're just talking about how **awesome** you are,' Kenny replied.

'Then don't whisper,' Charles said. **'Tell the world!'**

The clues and the river stopped suddenly at a giant rock face.

'It doesn't make sense,' Sarah said. 'Where did the animals go from here?'

'Maybe they climbed this cliff,' Kenny said.

'No way,' Billy Bob said. 'Wally's **terrified** of heights.'

I studied the rock face and noticed that a section of rock looked different to the rest.

'I think this is the entrance to a **cave,**' I said. 'But it's been blocked by a sheet of rock, which camouflages perfectly with the rest of the cliff.'

'I'll take care of it,' Charles announced.

He **pushed** and **heaved** but the sheet of rock didn't move.

'Doesn't look like **BRUTE FORCE** is the answer,' Tiffany said.

'This might be what we're looking for,' Sarah said.

She pressed a small black gemstone hidden in a crevice. The giant sheet of rock slid sideways, revealing an **enormous** cave.

'I was going to press on that gemstone,' Charles said.

As the six of us stepped inside, we quickly realised this was not your average cave. For a start, the walls were lined with art. And not the sort of art your little brother or sister creates at kindergarten. They were portraits that belonged in a gallery!

There was something about the portraits that made me feel **uneasy.**

We were inside a cave mansion, with dozens of rooms, each of them unique. One of the rooms was full of statues. Gold statues. Bronze statues. Clay statues. Statues of animals, mythological creatures and warriors.

'Hey, this **Viking guy** looks just like me!' Kenny said.

One room was full of **priceless artefacts** – the gloves of King Midas, a golden chariot, even the steering wheel of Noah's Ark!

Another room was full of **treasure** – jewellery, coins, pearls and diamonds.

'We're rich!' Kenny said, throwing a handful of gold coins in the air.

Kenny was only mucking around, but Charles stuffed an expensive-looking necklace, encrusted with jewels, into his pocket.

'What are you doing, Charles?' Sarah asked.

'That's **stealing,'** Tiffany added.

'Come on,' Charles replied. 'Whoever owns all this stuff can spare *one* necklace.'

'Even still,' I said. 'I don't think it's right.'

'Well, I **don't care** what any of you think,' Charles said. He stuffed a handful of gold coins into his other pocket.

The next room was crammed floor to ceiling with comic books. Some of the comics were incredibly **rare**, including the first-ever edition of Billy Bob's favourite comic-book series, ***POW POW PIG!***

'POW POW PIG!' yelled Billy Bob. 'You can keep your gold and jewellery, 'cos this is what I'm talking about!'

Billy Bob held the comic book aloft for a moment, and then carefully placed it back on its stand. He backed slowly away, with his head bowed.

As we continued walking through the cave, the river snaked alongside us. Then suddenly, above the sound of the burbling stream, we heard animal sounds.

Barking! Meowing!

Neighing! Chirping!

And something that sounded like a cross between a donkey and a duck.

We followed the animal sounds to a cavern in the centre of the cave.

'So this is Dr Kane's secret lair?' Kenny said.

'Must be,' I replied.

I always dreaded seeing Dr Kane. And I had a tummy full of **butterflies** about the possibility of seeing the **ULTIMATE NINJA** again, otherwise known as my dad.

Kenny and I peeked around the corner. This section of the cave was the most **impressive** of all. It had everything! Paintings. Statues. Jewellery. Weapons.

Giant crystal chandeliers hung from the roof and the floor was covered in gold mosaic tiles.

A red carpet running through the middle of the cavern led to an **enormous** throne.

Sitting on the throne was a gaunt man dressed in medieval armour.

My eyes were drawn to a **serpent ring** wrapped around his middle finger.

All of Duck Creek's pets were gathered around him, including **Noodles!**

I was deeply relieved to see her, even though she was at the feet of the **scariest** man I had ever seen.

'Wow, Dr Kane has **REALLY** changed!' said Kenny.

'That's not Dr Kane, Kenny,' I replied.

'Well, whoever he is, I recognise him from somewhere,' Kenny said. 'But I can't work out where . . .'

'The toys!' I announced. 'He was one of the **baddies** Dr Kane **brought to life** when he created the toy army!'

'Of course!' Kenny said. 'This guy must have **escaped** before we could turn him back into a toy.'

'It's **THE COLLECTOR!'** Sarah whispered as the others joined us.

'Well, obviously it's the Collector,' said Charles. 'Ummm, can you just explain who he is . . . for Billy Bob's sake?'

'The Golden Unicorn's nemesis,' Tiffany replied.

'I have **no idea** who you're talking about,' Billy Bob said.

'Shoosh! We can't let him see us,' Tiffany said.

Luckily, the Collector didn't hear us. He was more interested in all of the pets around him. Most of the animals were sitting or lying down, but some were doing tricks, including Noodles. She did a **spin.** She **rolled over.** Then she walked around on her hind legs like **a human!**

Noodles wasn't the only one doing tricks.

Tiffany's cat was **juggling!**

Charles' pony was dancing.

And Billy Bob's llama was doing **backflips!**

The Collector looked incredibly **menacing** with his metal armour and permanent scowl, but the animals seemed to love him. Especially two cute pugs that were snuggling into his feet.

As Sarah looked closer, she realised one of them was . . . **'Puggy!'**

'Don't worry,' I said. 'We'll get him back. We'll get them **all** back.'

EIGHT

'Tight huddle,' I said. We all bunched together outside the cavern.

'How are we going to get our pets back from the Collector?' Tiffany asked. 'He's **pure evil.**'

'He doesn't look like such a bad guy,' Charles said. 'Maybe we should just ask him *nicely*.'

'The Collector is greedy, selfish and insecure,' Sarah said.

'What's wrong with that?' said Charles. 'Maybe he's just misunderstood.'

'I'm telling you, the Collector won't give our pets back without a **fight**,' Sarah added.

'And if he **captures** us,' Tiffany said, 'he'll turn each of us into a portrait, like those above his throne.'

'**Whoa**,' Kenny said, staring at a portrait of a boy on the cavern wall. 'He can **turn people into portraits?!**'

Tiffany nodded.

'He gets all his power from the **MAGIC** ring on his finger,' Sarah said.

'He might be **evil,'** Charles said, 'but he really is an amazing collector. I've never seen so much **cool stuff!'**

'It's all stolen,' Tiffany said.

'And the Collector is never satisfied,' Sarah added. 'No matter how much he steals, he always wants more.'

'Including Wally!' Billy Bob said.

'Pets must be his new **obsession,'** Tiffany said.

'Why are our pets doing whatever the Collector tells them to?' Charles asked. 'Fancypants doesn't dance for me.'

'And I've never seen Wally do a backflip,' Billy Bob said.

'The Collector is **controlling** our pets using the ring,' Sarah said.

'How are a bunch of kids going to defeat an **evil wizard with a MAGIC ring?'** Billy Bob asked.

'With **NiNJA KiD** and **H-DUDE'S** help,' I whispered to Kenny.

'I'll leave it to you to explain our departure!' Kenny replied, darting into another section of the cave.

'Thanks,' I whispered. Then I turned to the others. 'Kenny and I are going to try to find a back way into the cavern.'

'I'll come with you,' Sarah said.

'Me too,' Tiffany added.

I gulped. This was not going well. 'Um . . . no, because . . . we need you to . . . keep a **lookout** from here,' I said. 'We'll be right back!'

I chased after Kenny.

Further into the cave, Kenny and I stumbled into a room full of shields, swords and other old weapons.

'Check this out!' Kenny said. He was studying a rack of **ENORMOUS** swords, forged of silver and steel.

'The Collector won't stand a chance once we're both wielding one of these!'

He tried to lift one of the swords but it was so **HEAVY**, Kenny fell to the ground.

We quickly changed into our **NiNJA KiD** and **H-DUDE** outfits.

'Is it just me,' I said, 'or is it getting **harder and harder** to hide our secret identities?'

'It's not just you,' Kenny said.

'I think we got away with it this time,' I said. 'By a whisker!'

We were interrupted by a **LOUD scream.**

It wasn't Sarah. Or Tiffany. Or Billy Bob.

'I'd know that scream anywhere!' Kenny said.

Kenny and I rushed back to the cavern entrance . . . but the others were **gone!** We peeked around the corner and were horrified by what we saw – the Collector had trapped them all in a **glass cage!**

'You distract the Collector,' I said to Kenny. 'I'll try to free them.'

'How am I going to distract him?' Kenny asked.

'With the old **H-DUDE charm!**' I replied.

Before I could even count us down, H-Dude burst into the cavern.

'Well, well, well,' Kenny announced happily. 'If it isn't the Collector! Excellent to see you again, good sir!'

'WHO ON EARTH ARE YOU?!' the Collector boomed.

'Such a joker!' Kenny said. 'How are things, old friend?'

'I **love** what you've done with the place,' Kenny said. He was pointing around the cavern as though checking out a newly renovated home.

As H-Dude kept the Collector busy, I quietly snuck into the cavern and made my way towards the glass cage.

I scanned all sides of the cage but there was nothing even resembling a door.

'There's no way out,' Sarah said.

'The Collector created the cage using his magical ring,' Billy Bob said.

'I want my mummy!' Charles said.

The Collector was losing patience with H-Dude. 'You've wasted enough of my time!' he bellowed. **'GUARD DOGS, ATTACK!'**

A pack of snarling Dobermans and Rottweilers **sprang up** and charged at Kenny.

I did a **double flip** and landed on top of the glass cage.

'H-Dude, up here! **Quickly!**'

The dogs were closing in on Kenny as he raced across the cavern.

'JUMP!' I yelled.

Kenny leapt and grabbed my hand. As I pulled him up, the guard dogs nipped at his heels.

'Let our friends and our pets go,' I yelled to the Collector.

'Your insolence is humorous,' he replied.

'I don't know what any of that means,' Kenny said. 'But you better do what Ninja Kid says, or this will get **messy.'**

'We can do this the **easy way** or the **hard way**,' I said.

'Let's try the hard way,' the Collector said, flashing an **evil grin.**

NiNE

The Collector pointed his magic ring at the chandelier above us. **CRACK!** It plummeted towards our heads!

Kenny and I jumped out of the way seconds before the chandelier **smashed** into a thousand pieces.

'Guards!' the Collector yelled.

'ATTACK!'

'I think living alone in a cave has made you go a **little batty,'** Kenny said. 'There are no guards here.'

'Are you sure?' the Collector replied. He pointed his ring at several armoured statues. They came to life and started **charging towards us!**

As the statues leapt onto the glass cage, I did a rapid **sweep kick**, sending two of them **crashing** to the tiles.

Meanwhile, Kenny threw himself at the feet of another guard, who tripped and **hurtled** headfirst into the ground.

The guards kept coming, but Kenny and I TWISTED, FLIPPED and KICKED until we'd beaten every single one of them.

Before we had a chance to catch our breath, the Collector aimed his all-powerful ring at a flock of pet birds hovering above his head.

'Finish them!' he yelled at the birds.

Parrots, crows, finches and cockatoos speared towards us as though they were fierce birds of prey.

'Get down low and **GO, GO, GO!'** Kenny yelled.

We both executed low rolls, narrowly avoiding the swooping birds.

'Feathered failures!' the Collector yelled at the birds. **'Llamas, attack!'**

Wally and several other llamas charged at us and started spitting violently. Kenny and I dodged and weaved all the flying spit.

The Collector was **not giving up**, and Kenny and I were no closer to releasing our friends from the glass cage. We hurried out of the cavern to regroup.

'Cowards!' the Collector called out after us.

'We need to come up with a Plan B,' I said.

'Or a **Plan C, D or E,'** Kenny replied. **'Anything** other than what we're doing!'

'The Collector gets all his power from that ring,' I said, 'so we need to **get it off** him.'

'How?' Kenny said. 'We can't even get close to him.'

'Not as humans . . .' I said.

'I see where this is going,' Kenny said.

'You happy to become **H-DOG** again?' I asked.

'Do I have a choice?' Kenny asked.

'Not really!'

'Then bring it on!'

'We need to lure Puggy out here first,' I said. 'Empty your pockets!'

Kenny still had a pancake in his pocket. 'Do I have to? I was **saving this** for later!'

Kenny held up the pancake so Puggy could see it. 'Here, Puggy, Puggy, Puggy!'

Puggy raced out to us, wagging his tail.

'Looks like the Collector's **MAGICAL** ring is no match for your mum's pancakes!' Kenny said.

As Puggy ate the pancake, I pointed the dog bracelet at Kenny. 'You know what to think about?'

'Sure do!' Kenny replied.

It worked! Now Kenny looked just like Puggy!

The real Puggy gave Kenny a strange look then continued **gobbling** up the pancake.

'Are you ready to become the Collector's best friend?' I asked H-Dog.

H-Dog did a little piddle on the tiles!

'I'll take that as **a yes.** You've got this, H-Dog!' I whispered.

H-Dog nodded, then scurried over to the Collector.

'There you are, my favourite little pooch,' the Collector said. He reached down to pat H-Dog.

H-Dog licked the Collector's hand . . .

then snatched the ring off his finger!

'HEY!' the Collector cried out. 'Give that back!'

H-Dog scurried over to me with the ring between his tiny teeth.

'Come back here, **you miserable mutt!'** the Collector yelled after him.

'Don't just stand there!' the Collector yelled at the other pets.

'Get my ring back!'

But all the animals completely **ignored** the Collector. Instead, Furball, Fancypants, Wally and Puggy raced over to the glass cage to see their owners.

Without the ring, the Collector's commands were **useless.** 'What are you doing, you foolish animals? **Obey your master!**'

I stepped out from where I was hiding. 'Release our friends,' I said to the Collector.

And just like that, the glass cage surrounding Sarah and the others **disappeared.**

'I was right,' Charles said. 'All you had to do was **ask nicely!**'

'I didn't want the cage to disappear, you fool!' the Collector yelled at him. 'It's the ring.' He turned to H-Dog. 'Give it back to me, you **pathetic pug**, before I lose **everything!**'

H-Dog poked his tongue out at the Collector and pranced around the cave!

Everything the Collector had stolen using the ring's evil magic began to disappear. The paintings. The statues. The jewels. The chandeliers. Even his throne.

'No, no, no!' the Collector screamed.

'Not my throne!'

'The Collector will have to change his name now that he's **lost** all of his belongings,' said Sarah.

'**The Loser** has a nice ring to it,' added Tiffany.

The necklace and coins that Charles had stolen also disappeared from his pockets. Charles couldn't believe it. 'That is **so unfair!**'

The Collector chased H-Dog around the cave. 'Get back here, you annoying mutt!' he yelled.

'Don't call him a mutt!' Tiffany said. 'He's **H-Dog!** And he's **AWESOME!**'

As the others cheered H-Dog on, he started getting cheekier. He rolled. He flipped. He walked on two legs.

But H-Dog's little legs were getting tired and the Collector was gaining on him. He was about to **pounce** on H-Dog when Sarah yelled out to Puggy.

'Give your fellow pug a hand!' she said.

'You too, Furball!' Tiffany said.

Puggy quickly tied the Collector's shoelaces together. And Furball jumped on the Collector's head.

The Collector couldn't see where he was going and he **tripped over** his laces and **CRASHED** to the ground!

'Don't mess with **pet power!**' Kenny said. He was so busy gloating, he **tripped** over his own little legs and the ring dropped out of his mouth . . .

. . . into the creek!

The ring was swiftly carried away by the raging waters.

'Goodbye, evil ring,' Kenny said.

'What have you done?!'

The Collector dived into the creek and swam after the ring.

'I'll get my ring back, even if I have to swim for weeks,' he yelled when he came up for air. 'And when I do,

I'll be BAAACCCKKKK!'

The rushing water of the creek swept him out of the cave.

'Goodbye, evil Collector,' Kenny said.

TEN

Everyone was hugging and patting their pets. I gave Noodles a huge hug. But the animal getting the most pats was **H-DOG!**

'H-Dog,' I said, 'you probably don't want to hear this, but I think it's time you returned to human form.'

'A little more patting,' Kenny replied. **'Please?!'**

Finally, H-Dog had had enough pats.

'Alright, Ninja Kid. Let's do this.'

I pointed Grandma's bracelet at H-Dog and counted, 'Four, three, two, one . . .'

'Wow,' I said. 'You really loved being H-Dog.'

'What's not to love? I thought I made a **paw-fect puppy!** But I still prefer being H-Dude.'

'I prefer you as H-Dude, too,' Tiffany said. 'Even though you were a super-cute pug!'

H-Dude blushed so brightly, he lit up the cave!

'We should get going,' I said.

'You're probably right,' Kenny agreed. 'Thanks for all your help, everyone. Especially Puggy and Furball. You guys saved my life!'

Sarah and Tiffany held their pets close.

'You guys were all **amazing**,' I said. 'Until next time!'

H-Dude and I pretended to go one way, then swiftly doubled back into the weapon room. We quickly changed and became plain old Nelson and Kenny once again.

'Alright,' I said to Kenny. 'Time for the Nelson-and-Kenny-miss-out-on-all-the-fun routine!'

'This bit's never easy,' Kenny replied.

'Sarah!' I called out. 'Tiffany! Where are you guys?'

'Charles!' Kenny yelled. 'Billy Bob! I think we're **seriously lost.**'

The others came rushing into the room, followed by the pets, including Noodles – who gave me and Kenny a **huge lick** on the cheek!

'Where have you been?' Sarah asked.

'Hiding as usual,' Charles said.

'We weren't hiding,' I said. 'We **got lost!** This cave is **huge!**'

'Did we miss anything?' Kenny asked.

'Ninja Kid and H-Dude took the Collector's ring and vanquished his power!' Sarah said.

'They were **incredible!'** Tiffany added.

'Those guys are **way cool,'** Billy Bob said.

'Let's get out of here,' Sarah said. 'This cave gives me **the creeps!©**

'Lead the way, Wally!' Billy Bob said.

Wally and the other pets trotted out of the cave, and the rest of us followed.

As we neared the end of the cave, Sarah's face lit up. **'No way!'**

She reached into the river and pulled out . . .

She pressed several buttons. 'It still works. Good as new!'

'Awesome!' Kenny said.

When we got back to Duck Creek, the pets **barked**, ***meowed***, **chirped** and **neighed** with excitement as they returned to their homes. At last, all of the pets were reunited with their owners, except for one . . . Noodles.

I looked at Kenny and knew, without saying a word, that we were thinking **exactly the same thing.**

ELEVEN

'Please can we keep her?!' Kenny and I begged Mum and Grandma.

Noodles wagged her tail excitedly.

'We haven't finished talking about the Collector,' Mum said.

'From now on, keep the Glove of Life with you at all times,' Grandma said. 'So if the Collector returns, you can turn him back into a toy.'

'I hope we **never** see him again,' I said.

'So do I,' Grandma replied. 'But I fear that's unlikely.'

'And we won't have seen the last of Dr Kane either,' Mum warned. 'He'll be back.'

'Great, so now we have **two crazy evil dudes** to deal with,' Kenny said.

'So back to the **big** question,' I said. 'Can we keep Noodles?'

'PLEEEEEASE?' Kenny pleaded.

Noodles wagged her tail and looked up at Mum and Grandma with her bright, kind eyes.

Mum and Grandma shared a look.

'Yes, you can keep her!'

'Woohoo!' I said.

'Let's make pancakes to celebrate,' Kenny said. 'They're Noodles' favourite.'

'I think they might be **your** favourite, too,' Mum said.

'Everyone wins!' Kenny announced.

READ THEM ALL!

NINJA KID 9

COMING SOON!